Understanding *Sopranos* Slang and Jersey Culture

A Guide to New Jersey Italian Lingo

By Danny Paul

Glossary

INTRODUCTION

I chose to write about myself to let everyone know why I wrote this book. So, I won't write in the third person. I am a Jersey boy by birth and in my heart - in the town of Ramsey to be exact. We do say Jersey and leave out the New. It's the only state with the word new in front of it where that can be applied - we feel that "New" is not necessary.

After watching the Sopranos, and even working on the set as an extra once, I realized that most people have no idea what Jersey Italian slang actually is. It is really not a big secret, it's just that the Italians that inhabit North Jersey destroyed not one, but two, languages. I guess a lot of cultures have experienced the same transition after a couple of generations away from the old country and are assimilating to the new. But it's really more than that actually; it's really just an attitude. A lot of words have different meanings depending on the context of the situation. I realized this growing up and began to apply it myself.

This book is not meant to be read like a novel; rather it is a handbook of sorts. I might provide the definition to the same slang word many times throughout the book, depending on context, and I feel that this makes it easier to cross reference. For example, if there's a particular scene you need insight on, and a word comes up that was explained in previous chapters, it will be explained again in its new context so that you don't have to constantly flip back to other scenes for reference.

I have been in the entertainment business for most of my adult life. I trained and toured as an improv comic and as a stand up comic. I have performed thousands of shows in all corners of the US and have always felt most at home coming back to the Northeast. While I was on the road I dabbled in writing for television and films but never had the interest to write a book. I guess you can call this more of a reference guide than a book. One avenue always leads to another in the entertainment business. That's why I eventually made my way into the television realm. I am not embarrassed to say I have appeared in everything from cheesy B-movies to over one hundred TV commercials. I was even a regular on a moderately successful home improvement show for a while called "In a Fix". I am very antsy by nature and am constantly striving to keep trying new and challenging endeavors.

Most people either "get" the Jersey attitude or they don't. Because of the success of the Sopranos, I believe people are generally more intrigued now by our little faction of society, so, I just felt the need to help explain it. I hope this little book will help you enjoy watching the show more and not end up being lost on those confusing Italian slang words. Understanding the attitude is something that nobody can explain, it just has to be experienced - so, I didn't attempt any psychological discourse on that. I will admit that I find New York City to be the most lively and exciting place in the world, yet I always find my way back to the Jersey shore to relax and unwind. I hope this book can help you relax and enjoy the show a little more. So let me just tell ya - you need to grab a slice and Fu- geh-da-bow-dit.

Thanks and Enjoy,

Danny Paul

The Complete First Season

On January 10th, 1999, America was introduced to two families that would make history: The Soprano family headed by Tony Soprano, and The Soprano "family" headed by Tony Soprano. Here's where it begins…

Season 1 Episode 1 - "The Sopranos"

In the kitchen of the Soprano house, Carmella asks Tony if he wants "left over ***shvoyadell*** from last night." It figures that the first thing I notice is a food item. This is a clam shaped layered pastry.

The boys are sitting outside Satriale's deli. Silvio tells the boys the reason he stopped by: "My uncle sent me here for the ***gabagoul***" (another food item). He is referring to an Italian cured meat, real name capicola, which is popular in northern American Italian homes. It makes a great hero sub sandwich with provolone cheese.

Carmella is talking to Tony while he is on the MRI table: "Having a ***goomar*** on the side doesn't help." This is the first of many times that she reminds Tony that she knows about his girl on the side. An Italian man who has a ***goomar*** makes sure that the girl on the side knows that he is a married man and she is a girlfriend only, and will never be more than a girlfriend.

In Dr. Melfi's office, Tony utters the word ***mafungu***. The way he uses it, he means, and here comes the "F" word, "ah, fuck you for thinking that."

Pussy and Chris are burying a dead body like they were delivering mail. Chris talks about ***whacking*** or ***wetting*** a body. The term ***whacking*** is used in many mob or Mafia movies. Yes, it means to kill someone. ***Wetting*** means the same thing, but is normally used when a body is dumped in the ocean or in a lake. Either word is interchangeable with the other. More exciting words for killing, are-a-comin'. In the same scene Chris says "Luka Braze ***sleeps with the fishes***." That was a direct quote from The Godfather I. In that movie it meant that poor Luka had been ***whacked***.

Tony in Dr. Melfi's office: "It used to be a guy got ***pinched***, he took his prison ***jolt*** no matter what." The word ***pinched*** means caught by the police or arrested. His prison ***jolt*** means a jolt of reality. A real man did his time in jail and shut his mouth.

We see Tony's boat for the first time. The name of the boat is ***Stugots***. This is a combination of two words ***stunade*** and ***oogots***. ***Stunade*** means stupid and ***oogots*** means nothing, zero, nada, nil - but put the two words together and it refers to having balls….. Yeah, me neither. The real meaning is, "this cock"

Chris on the phone with Tony: "***A friend of ours*** just got back in to town." In this case they don't want to use anyone's name on the phone. ***A friend of ours*** in Mafia circles means that the man is a made man. "***A friend of mine***" means that the man can be trusted.

Uncle Junior and Olivia in the car - Junior says: "But I'm all ***agida*** all the time." This has many meanings and I'm sure you will hear the rest. This time he is saying that his stomach is in knots over this subject.

Season 1 Episode 2 - "46 Long"

The boys in the back room are watching an ex-mob boss on TV. Paulie is upset at the mob boss telling all to the FBI. He calls him ***chacidone*** and in frustration he says ***ah finabla***. A ***chacidone*** is someone who talks too much. ***Finabla*** is like saying fuck you in a nice way.

Paulie and Pussy are in a Starbucks type coffee house and they don't have regular coffee. Paulie says "***Maduon***." This is a common reaction to something that can't be believed. It is like the Spanish "ah carumba," or "holy shit". It is not considered a curse word .

Tony and Olivia talk about Olivia's new house keeper. She is called a ***ditsoon***. The connotation is black or charcoal.

Season 1 Episode 3 - "Denial, Anger, Acceptance"

The original mob boss Jackie is dying of cancer in a hospital bed. His wife asks him if he needs anything. He says, "Bring me back some ***brojolle***." This is a beef cutlet rolled, stuffed and boiled in tomato sauce.

Silvio and Paulie visit the motel owned by the Hassidic Jew. The Jewish man is talking about his father-in-law: "I've known him since before there was hair on my ***pencil***." Yes, his ***pencil*** is a direct reference to his penis. Most cultures use a bigger, longer, circular object for a comparison to their family pride. Oy, if you're gonna lie to mobsters, why lie about that? Mashugina.

Artie and his wife Charmaine are in their restaurant's kitchen. Artie is talking about two people in the restaurant: "Two ***goombas*** from the ***old country***." Some people really don't know that a ***goomba*** is another Italian person that is a friend. The ***old country*** is Italy. Or did I have to mention that? You'd be surprised....

Season 1 Episode 4 - "Meadowlands"

Tony brings his mother a pastry box at the retirement community. Tony tells his mom that in the box is ***macaroons***. He brings cookies with powdered sugar.

The police detective waits outside of the retirement community to meet with Tony. Tony reminds him, "You're down ***two large***." This is a reference to a gambling debt - two thousand dollars. If you deal with a bookie, remember: a half is fifty, one dollar is one hundred, a nickel is five hundred, and a dime is one thousand or ***large***. Small is an amount under one dollar. Now, you got that? Go use an outside line.

In Jackie's hospital room: "A Moe Green special like in I." Tony was referring to Godfather I, where Moe Green was shot in the eye through his glasses. His day was ruined.

Tony and Uncle Junior talk in the restaurant. Junior talks about Tony's mom: "She's living like ***Povoetto*** in there." He means she is living like a poor person. And Junior also says, "He can give <u>you</u> ***agida*** for a change." Junior is telling Tony to deal with it. Junior continues: "I show you my ***hand*** and you slap it away." His ***hand*** is a way of saying that he shows him trust, or he shows his cards so he can decide to play or fold. Before Tony leaves, he is told by Junior: "The next time you come in here, you come in ***heavy*** or not at all." In other words, bring your gun because Junior means business.

The crew eats dinner and discusses family problems: "Raymond, go easy with the grease gun." He is saying don't push the subject. Don't make things harder by greasing the problem.

Season 1 Episode 5 - "College"

Meadow and Tony are on a road trip to review colleges. Meadow thinks her father is lying when he says, "Don't start ***milly-mouthing***." Yeah, like he can tell her how the business really works. Sorry kid.

Tony is on a pay phone with Chris talking about a man that he recognized. Tony thinks he might be an ex-mob boss who is in the witness protection program: "He flipped about ten years ago. He got busted for peddling ***H***." ***H*** is heroin, a real bad drug.

Again Tony is on the pay phone with Chris. This time Chris is dealing with a bad rain storm and has water in his shoes. "Tony, if you don't want to work in a water trap, work for the Yankees." If you are a baseball fan you know that they don't play in the rain. Apparently the players aren't paid enough.

Another pay phone visit in the rain for Chris... Chris wants to come up to Maine and kill the man that Tony found in the witness protection program. After Tony says, "don't come," Chris says, "***oogots*** don't come." Even though, ***oogots*** means nothing, literally, it is now used to say: that's crazy for me not to come.

Carmella and Father Phil are in the Soprano kitchen the next morning. "Of all the ***finook*** priests in the world, why did I get the one who's straight?" By saying that

Father Phil is straight, I believe the word ***finook*** is explained. Yes, it means gay.

Season 1 Episode 6 - "Pax Soprana"

Junior and Olivia are talking about coffee in the retirement home: "A magnet?" Junior talking about Tony: "You're looking to crack his ***colyaire*** for putting you in here." He means his neck.

Tony and Hesh talk on the sidewalk: "Ten cents out of every dollar for his kids comes directly from your ***shylock*** business. He's been boss ten minutes; he's givin' me ***agida*** already. How much does he want?" Hesh answers, "Five hundred ***large*** plus two points on my ***shy***." Well, here, Tony is upset because Junior doesn't appreciate ten percent of Hesh's loan sharking as it is. Then we find out that Junior wants five hundred thousand dollars up front and two percent of the business before Hesh's cut. That was easy enough.

Tony and Carmella are in the car, in the garage after their anniversary dinner. "You're the mother of my children. How can I ***shgeave*** you?" Carmella thinks that Tony finds her revolting to touch even though they are married. We know where he's really getting it.

The boys are sitting at the sidewalk table: "Hesh is not only a ***friend of yours***; he's a ***friend of ours***." Then Junior says, "Hold your cock when you do business with these desert people." Normally a mob guy will use the term, a ***friend of yours*** when the guy is not normally brought around, or, a made guy. The term a ***friend of ours*** means that he can be trusted and that he is a made man. In this case a ***friend of ours*** means that he just makes both of us money. He can't be a made man because he's not Italian.

Junior means to protect what's important to you when you deal with Jewish people. No offence to the desert people.

Tony brings Olivia cookies with almonds on top to her home. Olivia is in a hurry to leave. "I'm going downstairs before that ***kabruta*** activity lady finds me." She means that the activity lady is too pushy for her. Olivia is most likely too lazy.

Carmella and father Phil are in church talking about Tony's girlfriends. She says, "***sheafeotsa***, they mean nothing to Tony." ***Sheafeotsa*** means dirty and disgusting women - that gets to the point in just one word. Thanks Carmella.

Tony and Junior watch a baseball game. Junior remembers how good Tony could hit the ball as a kid: "You had a swing like Joe D." If you're not a baseball fan he meant Joe DiMaggio, the Yankee Clipper. Junior also sarcastically says, "You may be acting ***mental mortally***." Yep, like a retard.

Season 1 Episode 7 - "Down Neck"

At the Soprano dinner table Junior reacts to Tony's loud remarks: "He yells at me like a ***misawagawa***." He means a peasant that doesn't matter to him. You can't enjoy your food at an Italian dinner until someone yells.

In the back room at the pool table, Chris walks in: "I was picking up the chinaman's ***vig***." ***Vig*** is a percentage added to a gambling bet.

Tony's reaction to Chris's heist: "You fucking ***mamaluke***, you wanna spend eight years in prison?" He is calling Chris a dumb scumbag who doesn't think before he acts.

Tony and A.J. are changing a tire. Tony uses the word ***gagoots***. Gagoots is a way of saying that A.J is a little punk. The real word is from the word pumpkin or a type of squash.

Season 1 Episode 8 - "The Legend of Tennessee Mol Tisanti"

Jennifer Melfi's family discuses Italian misconceptions and they toast with wine: "***Chin don*** and ***salute***." ***Chin don*** is an expression that means "may you live for one hundred years."

In Chris's messy apartment, Paulie suggests that they get their ***joints capped***. If you didn't figure out the context, it means that they need to find some willing females. Not a bad idea when you're depressed. Badabing…

Tony talks to the Italian FBI agent after he breaks a bowl on his kitchen floor. Tony says in Italian: "***Grasso? de fracha culla cuzi***." Translation: "I'll break your ass."

The Soprano family discusses famous Italians that they are proud of. Tony mentions ***Frances Albert***. The last name is Sinatra. I couldn't believe that most non-Italians did not know this. That's just a crying shame. Frank is from Hoboken N.J. and when he left he never went back.

Season 1 Episode 9 - "Boca"

Uncle Junior is in bed with Roberta and talks about the fact that he is good at oral sex. He is worried that if the boys found out, they'd think "possibly that you're a ***finook***." He is afraid of the boys thinking he's a fag. That sure does explain a lot now.

In the restaurant Tony refers to the guy with a hat on as a ***sfvichachine***. This is like saying he is a sperm or a low life scum.

At the Soprano dinner table Junior says: "Olivia, I warned you, ***statazette***." Shut your mouth Olivia.

In the back room with the boys Silvio has a couple of beauties. "The man owes me a ***solid***," and "That's why she split her wrist, you ***stunod***." A solid is simply a big favor, and ***stunod*** means stupid. That's how you say it.

At the golf course Junior grabs Tony's cheek and says ***gwantizibella***. This happened to me my whole life and it is painful. Usually it was from a female in the family. It's like saying, "look at this beautiful face." A week with my Grandmother and my cheeks were hanging. She had some grip.

Still at the golf course but now on the T-box, Tony continues to bust Junior's balls. "I thought you were a ***bachalla*** man, why you eatin' sushi?" The real meaning is cod fish, a good slang word for pussy.

Season 1 Episode 10 - "A Hit is a Hit"

Chris tells Adrianna about the black rappers: "...but the ***moolis***, they got it going on." ***Moolinyan*** is the long version of this slang word that means a black and shinny eggplant. It is more often used to refer to African American people. It is an insult like the "N" word.

Hesh gives his opinion of a song as he and Chris listen to music in Hesh's office: "You pathetic ***schlepper***." This is more of a Yiddish word for a person who is slowly trying to get through life by being lazy.

Paulie is talking about the black rapper, Massive. "What kind of ***moolinyans*** are these?" Again the true meaning is a black and shinny eggplant.

Adrianna sits next to Chris in their apartment and asks, "***Eh cosi de gatzo***?" She wants to know if he wants it sucked.

Tony talks to his neighbor in the back yard and calls him ***Coozy***. It is short for his name, which is Cuzemano, but it is also refers to a woman's private parts.

Season 1 Episode 11 - "Nobody Knows Anything"

The FBI agent walks into a card game with his gun out: "If I wanted to bust up card games I'd have a doughnut in my mouth." I hope you understand that he is saying that this is just not an average police bust. It is also a great cop line.

Pussy complained when he got out of jail, "My head's hurting and I have ***agita***." I do believe he is complaining of heart burn. "They grabbed ***four dimes*** from me." That means they took the four thousand he had on him. Not the kind of cash a person normally carries.

The informant cop, Vinnie, gives Tony new information on the boat ramp: "Pussy is ***wired for sound***." He means that Pussy is wearing a listening device for the police.

Carmella brings Olivia ricotta pie. She says ***regutta*** pie. That's how we pronounce it, don't correct it.

Tony visits Pussy at his home. Pussy let's Tony know how bad he feels: "Some one put the ***melouyck*** on me." He thinks he may be cursed.

Tony and Silvio can't find Paulie. When he finally shows, he said he was at his ***goomar's***. This word comes up a lot so I have to repeat the meaning. He was at his girlfriend's house.

Season 1 Episode 12 - "Isabella"

Tony is at Dr. Melfi's office. He refers to a woman's private area when he says, "A gorgeous piece of ***cooze***."

Everyone is visiting at Tony's house. Carmella prepares a plate of food: "Silvio, ***gabagool*** over here." Capicola is sliced Italian cured luncheon meat and pronounced ***gabagool***.

Tony is on the phone with Dr. Melfi explaining that the girl he saw in his neighbors' back yard wasn't real; she was apparently a hallucination. When he asked his neighbor who she was, "He looked at me like I was fuckin' ***oobots***." Now, in my family we sometimes call people

skolobots. This is a colander for straining pasta. This slang means that you wear it on your head like a hat and implies that you have holes in your head. Tony, like many other Italians, just shortened the word to ***oobots***. Now it all makes sense…

Season 1 Episode 13 - "I Dream of Jeannie Cusamano"

Chris is in the elevator with Jimmy: "Tony's ***goomar*** is Russian." Once again, he is referring to Tony's girlfriend.

Olivia is in the Soprano house talking to Meadow after she is found wandering around: "Such a ***fache bruta***." Translation: Such an ugly face.

Carmella and Rosalita share a meal at Artie's restaurant. "Jackie's work is what killed him. All that ***agita*** gave him that disease." ***Agita*** can be many things, starting with heart burn. Some people believe that built up stress can cause cancer. I think it's true, so don't hold anything in.

The FBI takes Tony to listen to a tape recording of Junior. The agent reminds Tony, "You and I are not ***goombatta***." This is plural for ***goomba*** which means good buddy. It's hard to be close friends with the FBI.

Tony and Silvio discuss Chuck while at the pool table: "Tony, Chuck has to go away. I just passed my Coast Guard test." As you will see, Tony is just stating the method and place that Chuck will get it.

Tony returns to Dr. Melfi's office. He apologizes and speaks of fairness: "***Oogots*** fair, they don't care about fair." ***Oogots*** means nothing, so in this case it means ***fu-geh-da-bow-dit.*** So, ***fu- geh-da-bow-dit.***

At the Soprano dinner, Tony talks about A.J.: “Kids will be out of the house soon, even ***googots*** over here.” Literal translation: pumpkin, squash, or slang for dummy.

Father Phil misunderstands Carmella in the Soprano house: “I thought you liked movies, ***mea culpa***. You think I’m a ***shnora***, a parasite.” First he is saying, “It’s my fault” (mea culpa), and secondly, Priests shouldn’t use that kind of language referring to bugs… ***Shnora*** is actually a Yiddish word.

Artie opens the restaurant door as the Sopranos stand outside in the rain: “Ah, ***moduon***.” Again we find a word with many uses. Here he is saying, “Oh my God, what was I thinking? -come in from the rain.”

Still in the restaurant Silvio and Paulie quietly voice their opinions about Tony seeing a shrink. Silvio says, “***Besh boarno batuna***,” meaning that everything is fine.

The Complete Second Season

For Tony Soprano, there's no such thing as business as usual. Balancing the demands of his immediate family; wife Carmela, daughter Meadow and son Anthony Jr., with the demands of his other family; Paulie Walnuts, Silvio Dante and Big Pussy Bompensiero; means walking a tightrope no self-respecting mobster should ever have to walk. With his mother and uncle plotting against him, his older sister Janice wreaking her own special kind of havoc, and the very real threat that one of his closest allies is wired by the F.B.I, Tony needs the support of psychiatrist Dr. Melfi more than ever.

Season 2 Episode 1 - "A Guy Walks Into A Psychiatrist's Office..."

The episode opens with the Frank Sinatra song ***A Very Good Year***, and shows all the characters having a prosperous year. Tony is getting laid again… symbolic?

Pussy shows up at Tony's house after being missing for a while. Tony calls him a ***tan ghost***. This is a reference to Pussy being underground, but still oddly managing to get some sun while he was away. Pussy says, "They ***turn their hearts to stone***": meaning that his crew has turned their backs on him. He also says, "***There was a rap***," meaning that something was going down. The conversation turns to his back pain: "I was poppin' Percocets like they were ***Ju Ju Bees***." Ju Ju Bee's are a type of candy popular at the concession stand of a movie theatre. He's using the pain pills as an excuse for his erratic behavior. He then tells Tony, "I need to get my action back." In other words, he needs to get back in business. Tony gives Pussy a welcome back hug. Pussy takes it as a frisk for a gun. He grabs his manhood: "Do you want to pat this down too?" The conversation turns to Uncle Junior: "So who was in charge of screwing Junior?" That not only infers that Junior is getting screwed, but that someone was officially given permission to do it.

Tony meets with his lawyer in the back room of the Bing. The lawyer tells Tony, "You're gonna have to put up bigger ***blinds***." He wasn't talking about window coverings. The word ***blind*** is used as it would be in a "Texas hold 'em" poker game. In the game, a small pre bet to the hand is known as a blind. Tony responds: "The only way to run a business is bunker style;" making a comparison to the military which he does often. He needs to watch his surroundings more.

All the boys are together in the back room for the first time. Sil puts everyone in stitches with "Just when I'm out, they pull me back in," and "Alright Kay, just this once you can ask me about my affairs," and "Our true enemy has yet to reveal himself." For the very few people who don't watch mob movies; these are all attempts at a Godfather impression, one from each Godfather movie. Apparently Sil' is the Rich Little of organized crime.

Tony and Janice are sitting by the pool. Janice asks Tony for money for their mother's assisted living facility. Tony responds "Ma is ***on the lam*** in that hospital." The expression, ***on the lam***, is used a lot. It always refers to someone going somewhere to hide out until all is well enough to come back without harm. In this case, their mother is hiding from being responsible for her own health, and other things…

Carmella and her mother are preparing food in the kitchen. Carmella's mother sends her husband to the market and tells him to pick up some ***bosinagol***. Lots of Italian foods are mentioned that the rest of the country has no clue as to what they are. ***Bosinagol*** is basil, an herb.

The crew tells stories around Tony's outdoor patio barbeque. Sil' says, "We flew first class on the plane - ***fuh-geh-da-bow-dit***," referring to Donnie Brasco, the 1997 film starring Al Pacino. That is the best example I've ever heard for the word ***fuhgehdabowdit***.

Season 2 Episode 2 - "Do Not Resuscitate"

Not all shows are full of slang that most of the country has to figure out or ask their Italian friends about. This sure is one of 'em…

Tony and Bobby talk about the fate of Junior's share of the business. After Tony lists exactly what he will take and what Uncle Junior is going to get he says: "Uncle Junior can keep his ***stripes***." Again Tony makes a reference to the military. He means that Uncle Junior retains his status as mob boss.

Tony and Uncle Junior meet in the sound secure doctor's office. This is Uncle Junior's meeting room. Tony was upset that he had to tell the same stuff to Uncle Junior that he told Bobby: "I never would have talked to that ***calzone*** with legs." Tony, without a doubt, is talking about Bobby's weight. A ***calzone*** is another Italian food. Often tasty, a ***calzone*** is sort of a folded over pizza with ricotta cheese inside. If you have the means, I highly recommend it the next time you consider a Jersey pizza.

Season 2 Episode 3 - "Toodle-Fucking-Do"

Richie and Tony meet in the mall and Richie reminds Tony that he saved him from getting killed: "I'm the one who saved you from the hit parade."

Janice visits in Olivia's hospital room. Janice says, "***Ah fuma statazett***." Janice wants Olivia to please be quiet.

Season 2 Episode 4 - "Commmendatori"

In the party store, Pussy talks to the FBI about Chris: "Their talking like this Moltisanti kid might get his ***button***." He's letting the FBI know that Chris may soon become a made man.

Rosalie, Carmella and Angie are in the restaurant talking about Pussy's return. Rosalie yells to the next table, "Fucking nosey, eat your ***Manigut***." That is the Italian way to pronounce Manicotti. What do we know?

Paulie's in his hotel room with an Italian hooker: "There's my little ***fragalene***." Hey, it's my little fragile girl.

Season 2 Episode 5 - "Big Girls Don't Cry"

In Artie's kitchen, Tony asks to place one of his men in the restaurant. Artie is not sure what to say….. "Does he know his ass from ***shcamutz***?" He wants to know if he is smarter then ass cheese.

Tony talks about his bad temper and the good old days at Hesh's house: "You never saw ***Carlo***, or ***Lucky*** or Douglass McArthur going around punching walls." Carlo Gambini and Lucky Luciano are the other two leaders he was referring to.

Season 2 Episode 6 - "The Happy Wanderer"

Tony peeing in the men's room with David: "I figured you for the ***trotters***." Tony assumed that David liked to bet on the horses.

Vito at the poker table: "One chip, ***hava nablie***, can't even buy McDonalds with that." One chip, that's beautiful.

Richie picks up an envelope at the sporting goods store from David: "That envelope is ***two C's*** shy." David wants Richie to know that it's two thousand less then he owes.

Paulie gets pulled over and points a gun at the cop's crotch. "If I shoot, it's going in your ***brogolli***." The real meaning is a type of meat. A woman can also be a nice ***brogolli***.

Tony and Chris at the executive poker game: "Give him five ***boxes of ziti***." If you pay attention to the rest of the game, it becomes obvious that a ***box of ziti*** is one thousand dollars, but that is the slang for poker chips and not too commonly used....maybe because not many people can throw around that much ziti.

Still at the poker game Silvio is freaking out: "I should have stayed at my ***goomar's*** tonight." He thinks he would have been better off at his girl friend's house.

Tony at the funeral home referring to Janice, Richie and Olivia: "***Me fongul etu***." Well, fuck me. That explains it.

Season 2 Episode 7 - "D-Girl"

Chris and his cousin Greg hug at a bar: "***Facha brut***." This is a nice affectionate way of saying "fuck you."

Chris and Janeane Garofalo talk outside the movie set. Chris is upset that a story in his script has been stolen and used by someone: "That fucking, cock sucking, ***mensi fanook***." This means, fag mouth.

Chris in the hotel lobby with Amy: "Do you want to see me get ***clipped***?" Chris didn't mean, "Come and see me get a hair cut." ***Clipped*** is another way of saying whacked.

Pussy hugs Tony at A.J.'s confirmation party: "***Sobada di***." He means, "God bless you," but in this instance it's like saying goodbye.

Season 2 Episode 8 - "Full Leather Jacket"

Carmella talks over the fence to her neighbor about Meadows letter. Berkeley, ***modoun***, Berkeley." This word has many meanings. In this case it means, "Oh my God."

Richie gets a visit from Chris's boys and they refer to him as ***homey***. Richie's reaction is not pleasant. "If you wanna talk like a moolinyan, I'll send you to ***slip and fall school***." Richie lets the boys know that if they want to use lingo from the hood, they shouldn't use it around him, or he'll drop 'em.

Dinner at the Soprano house: A.J. asks his grandpa if he wants to play after dinner. Grandpa responds, "***Ooh fah***." His grandfather is just saying "uh oh," or "oh fuck" in a nice way.

Carmella brings a pie into her neighbor's sister's law office. "I brought you a ricotta pie." Italians say ***regutta***. Don't ask.

Season 2 Episode 9 - "From Where to Eternity"

Richie talks to Tony outside the hospital: "Tommy Biondi from ***OTB*** came up with a name." For the non gamblers, that's an acronym for off track betting.

Gabriella talks to Carmella in the hospital waiting room: "Ralph has had his Brazilian ***goomar*** for years." Again, we even see the women calling the men's girlfriends ***goomar***.

Tony talks in Dr. Melfi's office: "The Hitlers, the ***Pol Pots***, they deserve to go to hell." ***Pol Pot***, otherwise known as Saloth Sar, (May 19, 1925 - April 16, 1998) was the ruler of the Khmer Rouge and the Prime Minister of Cambodia...not to mention an evil despot...

Big Pussy mentions a ***Gabagool*** sandwich to the FBI agent in the car. He, of course, is referring to the Italian meat, capicola.

Season 2 Episode 10 - "Bust Out"

The boys are doing business at the Ramsey Outdoor store. Tony sees Pussy come in to the store: "There they are, the ***flying Gavone brothers***." This is Tony's way of saying "hey, how ya doin' you scumbag." The people who grew up in Ramsey N.J., like me, call it Ramsey Indoor Outdoor store. My brother worked there for a short time. Also in the Ramsey Outdoor store Tony remarks: "Five minutes away from fucking ***camp*** and I'm laughing." When Tony refers to camp he is not talking about roasting marshmallows around a fire. He means prison… you know, the big house.

Tony talks to A.J who's carrying a fishing pole: "Hey, ***gagoots.***" ***Gagoots*** has many meanings. When Tony says it to A.J. it's like saying, "hey you punk kid."

Season 2 Episode 11 - "House Arrest"

Katherine, the woman from the hospital, brings manicotti to Uncle Junior's house. She pronounces it ***Manigut***.

Junior, under house arrest, responds to Bobby asking him why he won't talk to Katherine: "Talking to that ***drednore*** wouldn't help." A ***drednore*** is someone who just brings you down by being around them.

Tony at a party on the golf course talks to Richie: "Are you ***stunod*** or what?" This has many meanings, but in this case it just means stupid.

Pussy jokes with the German helmet on: "I know nothing." I just hope you didn't miss this reference to the great sitcom character, Shultz, of Hogan's Hero's fame - a great television show that the Soprano crew would have grown up watching.

Tony walks in the crew's back room and hugs Chris: "How's the clay pigeon?" Tony is saying that Chris is an easy target.

Season 2 Episode 12 - "The Night In White Satin"

Junior talks to his lawyer in the law office: "I'm hem ridging ***sponyewlics*** here." He also says, "yeah, Wrigley fucking field." First, Junior is making sure that the lawyer knows that his guts are bleeding just from listening to him. Second, Junior wants a ball park figure as to how much the lawyer's fees will be. Wrigley Field is the baseball park where the Cubs play.

Junior talks to Bobby about Richie as Richie walks away: "He's got tremendous ***moxey*** for his size." Moxey was a term used in the N.Y. Tri-State area in the 50's and 60's. It has lots of meanings but it is mostly used to describe a guy with a lot of balls - perfect for Richie.

Janice talks about the wedding planner at her engagement party. "My planner did Rick Cerone's wedding." Rick Cerone was a catcher for the N.Y. Yankees the season after the death of the great Thurman Munson.

At the same engagement party, Janice sounds relieved: "I have been looking for my soul mate all my life, ***modoun***." As we know, this word has many meanings. Here it is a verbal sigh of relief.

Carmella reflects as Janice tries on her wedding dress: "In a year, tops, you're gonna have to deal with a ***goomar***." Carmella reminds her that eventually all the mob guys get a girlfriend on the side. They are just being human. That is a great line from the movie, "I Love You To Death".

Tony talks to Junior in his safe doctor's office: "You're like a double agent; fuckin' ***Matt Helm***." The great Dean Martin made a series of spy movies as the character Matt Helm. A man from the 50's looking cool in the 60's… only Dino could do that.

Richie talks about his son to Janice in their house: "He carries my ***discottiodi***." This means a man's legacy.

Season 2 Episode 13 - "Funhouse"

Tony slides money into Silvio's coat at the restaurant: "Ah, ***modoun.***" This time, the word expresses surprise; Silvio is shocked at the huge amount of money in the envelope.

In Artie's restaurant Silvio discusses the food and what's in it: "It's stuffed with ricotta." The North Jersey Italians say it differently.

Still in the restaurant, Artie and Silvio talk about their daughter's experience being on the soccer team at school: "Heather didn't walk away with ***oogots***." Artie is saying that at least Silvio's daughter benefited from it, but his daughter walked away with nothing.

Pussy talks about money in the F.B.I. car: "President Franklin is my best friend." He is talking about 100 dollar bills. Even though he's on the 100 dollar bill; Ben Franklin was never a president. He couldn't run because he had 33 kids out of wedlock. Now <u>that's</u> how he discovered electricity.

In Tony's bedroom, Artie talks about the mussels that Tony ate: "***Whoa Nelly***, I pick every piece of shellfish myself." The term ***Whoa Nelly*** is like saying, "slow down horsey."

Tony, at Pussy's front door, talks with Angie. "Aw ***modoun***, my poor ass." Tony is letting her know that he was in serious pain.

Pussy says hello to Silvio in his bedroom. "Hopalong ***gesiteche***, how you doin?" That's like saying, "what the news?" from Tony's side kick, sort of-ish. (This is a reference to Hopalong Cassidy - the great character of Western movies.)

On the boat, Pussy tells the boys about information he has been telling the F.B.I.: "Little things, picayune shit." In other words, he's saying that he's not telling them anything of great importance.

At Meadows graduation party, Tony pulls Chris aside: "I'm proposing you get your button". Tony is letting the other bosses know that it is time for Chris to become a made man and be in the mob for life. Sounds so final…

The Complete Third Season

Some suburban households have two cars. Some have two houses. But Tony Soprano has two families. This could be why the FBI is going to such lengths to wiretap his home. It may be also why the son of his dear late friend Jackie Aprile is causing him such agita - and why a Russian housekeeper is searching for her missing leg - and why his son is vandalizing school property - and his daughter is getting her heart broken - and also why his wife Carmela is both consulting a psychiatrist and confessing to a priest, and it's also why Tony Soprano is still seeing Dr. Melfi for his anxiety attacks.

It isn't easy heading-up the mob in New Jersey, but that's what puts dinner on the table for the two families of Tony Soprano.

Season 3 Episode 1 - "Mr. Ruggerio's Neighborhood"

Tony sitting at the table having lunch with the boys: "You're not hungry? - have some ***brojolli***." This word has many, many meanings. In this case it is just an edible meat item. He just says it in the Italian way.

Still at the table, Furio chimes in: "Yo ***gatabesht***, you are a twin brother." This means, "oh, I get it now."

Still at the same table, Tony jokes: "***Stunod***, it's a joke, come on." ***Stunod*** is a way of saying, "hey, stupid."

Tony speaks of the dead twin brother: "And your brother, ***bone manna***." Tony is saying, "With all due respect".

Season 3 Episode 2 - "Proshal Livushka"

Tony talks to Meadow's friend Noel about being black: "***Ditsoon***, charcoal briquette, ***moolinyan***." Again, ***moolinyan*** or ***mooli*** means eggplant but is used to describe black people.

In the funeral home, the undertaker Cozerelli quotes a classic line from The Godfather: "I'll use all my powers, all my skills." The undertaker listened to the same line from Vito Corlione about his son, Sonny.

Season 3 Episode 3 - "Fortunate"

At Chris's party after becoming a made man, Carmine reminisces about the old days: "There is no ***stigmata*** these days." He means that you don't have to go through as much pain and suffering as you did in the old days to become a made man. He believes that Chris has not yet paid his dues. (Stigma is what Carmine meant to say - stigmata refer to the crucifixion marks of Jesus on the cross).

In the pizza parlor after Chris was made - Dino, Jackie's friend, kisses a little ass: "Good to see you Chris, keep ***dino amad***." He means don't forget about me.

In Dr Melfi's office, Tony talks of Meadow's friend: "I told Buckwheat to stay away from my daughter." He is comparing the African American kid to the Little Rascals character Buckwheat, a hilarious character brought back to us by Eddie Murphy on SNL in the 80's. Now, that's funny.

Still in the doctor's office, Tony talks about fainting: "I was getting the ***gabagool*** out of the refrigerator." He means capicola, the Italian lunch meat.

While barbequing, Tony talks to Chris about Jackie's relationship with Dino: "Why is Jackie hangin' out with that ***moothidell***?" Tony thinks that Jackie is better than Dino. He is calling Dino a low life, starving to death, scumbag that he can't trust.

Tony is in the stands at A.J.'s football game: "4th and 3rd and this ***shadrool*** is going for it." ***Shadrool*** means a stupid person or literally a cucumber head.

Tony and A.J. sit on the couch watching football. Carmella talks about Meadow. Tony says, "This is about ***Sambo***, huh." Again Tony finds another racial slur to refer to black people. ***Sambo*** is a derogatory term that harkens back to the slave days. I don't think Tony cares.

Season 3 Episode 4 - "Employee Of The Month"

Tony and Furio pull up to the outside of Lodi Pizza and Ralphie sees them: "***Modoun***, look at this pair. So, how many Neapolitans does it take to screw in a light bulb? Use that on your ***pisans***." The use of this condescending joke is translated as saying - "Holy shit, these two people don't belong together even though they are both from Naples. Between the two of them they couldn't even screw in a light bulb. So, use that on your friends."

Sil' and Tony are in the back of the Bing: "Tony, cut off his ***gazzis***'." He's referring to a man's package. ***Gazzi*** literally means pig meat or even a bike tire.

John walks into the back room of the Bada Bing: "Is that all you guys talk about is ***cooze***?" This is slang for pussy.

In the back of the Bada Bing, Silvio talks about a lot of money: "25 million, ***modoun a mia***." Oh mama, that's a lot of money.

In the Soprano house, Jackie hears Tony talk about Meadow's black friend: "Don't worry Ton', I won't say anything about the ***moolinyan***."

Season 3 Episode 5 - "Another Toothpick"

In Dr. Melfi's office, Carmella and Tony see Melfi together for the first time. Tony: "I told you about the ***gabagoul*** and my mother when I was a kid." He means capicola meat.

Tony and Carmella in the car getting a speeding ticket - Tony: "Can you believe this? This ***smoke*** is actually writing me up." Smoke has a double meaning: Smoke, as in "Smokey and the Bandit" and smoke, as in slang for a black person.

Tony is outside the church talking about Bobby's father: "Lung cancer, oh fuck, ***modoun***." In this case ***modoun*** means: "This is serious."

In Artie's restaurant, Tony listens to Artie confess his love for Adriana. Tony says, "You can have hair like Casey Kasem, it won't make a difference." For many years Casey was a radio and television DJ that was famous for presenting the weekly top 40. He had a thick, full head of hair. It almost looked like a toupee. Keep your feet on the ground and keep reaching for the stars….

In Artie's restaurant Ralphie talks about Bobby's father: "My man ***gagootz***, he knows what he's doin' hah."

The word ***gagootz*** is normally used to talk about some one as if they were a punk. In this case he means that the man is old and is in his second childhood. He is done paying his life's dues.

Season 3 Episode 6 - "University"

In the Soprano kitchen, Tony tells Carmella about Meadow's black friend: "See how I didn't rise to the bait, the ***moolinyan***." Again, meaning the eggplant or the black kid.

In the champagne room at the Bada Bing, Silvio tells the guys what he thinks of Ralphie. "Ah ***stunod***, this guy." How stupid can he get?

Silvio and Tony talk about the stripper at the Badabing. "Ah ***modoun***, those choppers, what a train wreck." He is saying, "Oh my God, her braces are ugly."

At Ralphie's apartment Tracey gets an ear full from Silvio: "***Scotsioda*** you have a little kid at home." He is saying, what are you thinking? You could break up your family over this.

Behind the Bada Bing, Tony hits Ralphie for killing Tracey. "Are you crazy laying your hands on me? I'm a ***made guy***." Ralphie is saying that a made guy is untouchable and cannot be messed with without permission from all the heads of the families.

Season 3 Episode 7 - "Second Opinion"

Chris is in his apartment and tells Adriana about Paulie: ".....except for that ***scachone*** Paulie." He's calling Paulie a bastard, or a bitch.

Tony and Junior are in the elevator at the doctors' office. "Let me ask you about this JFK worship. What about Hoffa and the teamsters?" Tony is referring to Jimmy Hoffa, the former head of the Teamsters Union, who Bobby Kennedy wanted behind bars.

Junior and Tony are in Junior's house: "I sent him a box of ***Cohibas***." These are fine Cuban cigars - illegal to possess in America.

Season 3 Episode 8 - "He Has Risen"

Paulie talks about Ralphie at the craps table: "Fucking ***fachedemeer***, he don't say hello?" He is calling him a shit faced person. When it is said in Italian, it is not a joke.

Sil' and Tony discuss the dead stripper at the restaurant. Sil' says, "She was not your ***goomar***." He reminds Tony that the girl was not his girlfriend and he has no right to judge Ralphie for what he did.

At the Bada Bing, Silvio talks about Thanksgiving dinner: "***Modoun***, who needs it?" In this case modoun means "what a pain in the ass."

Tony tells Dr Melfi what he would do to Ralphie: "Normally I would put him out to pasture." He means he would kill him without question.

Rosalie talks to Ralphie at their Thanksgiving dinner: "You hardly touched your ***manigutt***." They ate manicotti for Thanksgiving. That's supposed to be before the bird.

Paulie tells the guys about Ralphie while at the card table: "You hear? Tony invited Ralphie to Thanksgiving, ***modoun***." In this case ***modoun*** means that this can be trouble.

At the poker table, Gigi holds his stomach: "Turkey, it's like ***shpackal*** in my bowels." He feels like his stomach wall is busting open.

Tony arrives at Junior's house: "Leftover turkey and ***manigutt***." Turkey and manicotti is a great holiday combination.

Junior talks about Ralphie to Tony. "A real ***contrimise*** you got on your hands, he's a real ***drabalene***." He is calling him a big dick that causes controversy.

Paulie talks about his associate dying while on the toilet: "On the ***bishadoon***, fucking humiliating." This is a word for a public toilet.

Season 3 Episode 9 - "The Telltale Moozadell"

Furio and Rocko at the bar in the Lollipop Club: "Ah ***modoun***, give him a drink." In this case ***modoun*** means: okay, enough.

Carmella and Rosalie try some new food at Artie's restaurant: "It tastes like ***mutsilell*** and beans to me." She means mozzarella cheese.

Still at Artie's, Rosalie and Carmella talk about how Artie may be getting divorced: "Artie's marriage is in the ***pishadoo***." ***Pishadoo*** is Italian slang for toilet.

In the parking lot at the car dealership, Gloria tells Tony she has to return to work by saying, ***Trabajar***. ***Trabajar*** means work in Spanish.

Tony walks into the back door at the casino. "***Como esta*** gentlemen?" or, how're you doing guys.

At the Baba Bing bar Jackie kisses Chris's ass a little: "I only have admiration for you since you got your button." He has respect since Chris has become a made guy.

Season 3 Episode 10 - "Save Us All From Satan's Power"

On the boardwalk, Tony recalls a conversation he had with Pussy: "Don't be moving that ***H*** no more, too risky." ***H*** is heroin.

On the boardwalk, Paulie: "He's in to me for 100 ***large*** on basketball." 100 large is really large. In gambling terms it means 100 thousand.

In the bedroom, Carmella refers to Janice's horrible cooking skills: "I'm doing Christmas eve. You wanna turn *her* loose on shellfish?" The reason that Carmella is worried about Janice cooking shellfish on Christmas Eve is because it is an Italian tradition to have shellfish on Christmas Eve and she doesn't want Janice to mess it up.

Tony has a flashback about Pussy and remembers Pussy making an excuse: "My ***goomar***'s mother was in the hospital all night." There is no way to validate the whereabouts of Pussy's girlfriend, or ***goomar***.

In Artie's restaurant, Paulie talks about Christmas: "What are you getting your ***goomar*** for Christmas?" He's asking, "Are you getting your girlfriend a present?"

At the restaurant table, Sil' sees Charmaine: "Ooh ***modoun***, look who it is." He is saying that Charmaine is looking good to him.

Tony orders a drink at the bar: "Wild Turkey, neat." In the old days when someone wanted a shot of liquor without ice, it was ordered: "neat". I'm not sure if modern day bartenders even know that.

Season 3 Episode 11 - "Pine Barrens"

At the Pine Barrens Chris is being sarcastic with Paulie: "***Bruno Magli*** over here." He compares Paulie to a famous men's footwear designer - he's wearing fancy shoes in the middle of the woods, of all places.

In the woods at Pine Barrens, Bobby shows his Jersey knowledge: "A lot of strange people used to live in these woods, Jackson Whites - these weird albinos" - well, this was part of the inspiration for writing this book. Bobby shows he knows Jersey well when he talks about the Jersey mountain people. That's right, North Jersey hillbillies. I heard lots of stories from people in the town I grew up in and from my uncle Tony. They all agreed that the mountains of North Jersey were inhabited by inbred mountain people that never let anyone on their hill. They lived with no running water and no electricity. Legend has it, that if you go up the mountain, even by accident, you don't come out. There is a story of a police officer, among many people, that met that fate. I've only heard of the Jackson Whites in the north Jersey mountains. Even most people that have been born and raised in Jersey don't know about this legend. In this episode, the Soprano writers mention that strange groups of inbred albinos lived off of exit 12. That is actually way down south.... but who knows. So, don't be scared of the bears. Be scared of the people who have been there longer then time itself.

Season 3 Episode 12 - "Amour Fou"

Angie asks Ro how her calamari is at the restaurant: "How's your ***galimar***?"

Carlo threatens Gloria in the car: "You stay away from Tony Soprano, ***gabesh***?" This is actually a bastardization of the Italian word ***capisce*** - meaning "do you understand?"

Season 3 Episode 13 - "The Army Of One"

Paulie's mother, Nucci, is paranoid in the retirement home: "Aw, ***modoun*** a mia. They don't eat snails do they?" In this instance, ***modoun*** means that she couldn't stomach it if it was true.

Ralphie reminds us how tough he can be: "I'm gonna give that little fuck a mass." He doesn't mean that he will take him to church. Ralphie shows us the Italian Jersey slang for some one who is about to receive a large amount of hurt.

Paulie is at the outdoor meeting and he talks about Jackie Jr.: "You deserve ***oogatz***." Or, you get nothing, spit, empty.

Chris and Tony talk about Jackie Jr. at the funeral home. "I'm sorry the guy was ***moushadare***." This is someone who flies off by himself.

At the outdoor sit down with Tony, Paulie complains: "***Che puzz***, I almost puked." ***Che puzz*** means "what a stink."

Furio slips, falls down and screams: ***Svachie***! This could be short for Svacchandanath, a Hindu deity. Perhaps Furio, being superstitious, believes some strange, unseen force caused him to slip and fall….

Adriana and Danielle meet at the shoe store. Adriana talks about her feet: "Ah ***modoun***, Jesus." Well, we know who Jesus was; modoun here means the same thing as Adriana complains about her aching feet.

Tony talks about A.J. in his military uniform: "Ooh, ***Sergeant Bilko***." This was the title of a very funny black and white TV sit-com starring the very funny Phil Silvers. This military comedy was later made into a movie with Steve Martin.

Paulie talks to John in the parking lot: "Since Ralphie is bringing his ***espinnoge shadole***, you think I was carrying a load in my pants. He is saying that Ralphie is full of cash, and that Paulie is full of shit.

The Complete Fourth Season

It's tough times in Jersey for Tony Soprano. The sluggish economy hasn't been good for the family business. His wife Carmela is angling for more financial security. Some long time lieutenants aren't happy with Tony's recent decisions. A rival boss wants a bigger piece of the suburban pie. A Soprano is heading to trial for the first time in decades. At least one child seems to have lost interest in higher education, and the ducks aren't coming back anytime soon.

Season 4 Episode 1 - "For All Debts Public and Private"

Junior meets with Tony at Junior's doctor's office: "My legal problems have let you go around like a ***gabavreche***." A ***gabavreche*** is a murderer with no conscience. Junior is inferring that Tony is "getting away with murder" while Junior is handcuffed by his legal predicament.

Tony makes a wisecrack to Ralphie at the dinner table: "Bruce Dern, don't you got somewhere to be?" Tony is referring to the well known actor who rose to fame for his roles in a few cheesy motorcycle movies produced in the late 60's.

Janice is in the bathroom with Ralphie talking about Ro': "Ah ***Bartleby***, ah humanity." Janice is quoting the key line of a famous short story by Herman Melville, "Bartleby," because it indicates that the image of Bartleby stands as a symbol for humanity on a universal level. This is Janice's sarcastic way of saying that Ro' is being overly dramatic.

Ro shows the F.B.I agent, Danielle, the Soprano house: "Danielle did you see the ***loggia***?" ***Loggia*** is the name given to an architectural feature, originally of Italian design, which is often a corridor, generally on the ground level, supported by columns or pierced openings in the wall.

Junior flirts with the nurse at the doctor's office: "***Una bella giornata*** to the city called Atlantic." He'd like to take her to Atlantic City….

Junior gets mad in his kitchen: "Why don't you go on ***Joe Franklin*** and tell the whole tri-state area." Joe Franklin is a cheesy local talk show host that has been in the N.Y. and N.J. area since before there was television.

Junior talks to Tony in the kitchen about the nurse being an agent: "A young ***cooze*** smiled at me and birds started chirping." Once again, he is referring to a piece of pussy.

Season 4 Episode 2 - "No Show"

Chris is in the back office of the Crazy Horse with Adriana, scolding her about Danielle, the FBI agent: "What have I been telling you about this ***pucchiachia***?" This is a derogatory way of saying pussy, or worse - cunt….

The FBI agents talk about what to do with Danielle: "Hire only ***schifosas***." A ***schifosa*** is an unattractive woman.

Season 4 Episode 3 - "Christopher"

Carmella thanks Furio for the food: "Thank you for bringing the ***stufoli***. I love those." I proudly grew up eating ***stufoli*** on holidays. They are small hard dough balls covered in honey and sometimes colored sprinkles.

In the Soprano kitchen, Carmella asks Tony if he is feeling well: "You okay Tony? You look a little ***muscia-moush***." She is saying half good and half bad.

The female speaker at the Italian American woman's club raises a point: "The world sees us as pizza makers and ***Mama Leones***." The term ***Mama Leone*** is used to talk about a woman that is made into a homemaker wife who is uneducated and has no say in her husband's business affairs. She continues: "We're from the land of aromatic ***Asiago*** and supple ***Barolo***. If they say spaghetti and meatballs, you tell them ***Orecchiette*** and broccoli rabe." She is referring to aromatic cheese, fine wine, and small, delicate pasta.

Sil is giving his opinion to Tony in the back room of the Bing: "I pay money to the anti- defamation coordination council, and ***basta***." Sil is saying he has had enough already.

Ralphie talks to the Indians about the poster of Del Redclay: "The guy is a total ***fugace***." He means that he is a total fake or phony.

Sil's wife Gabriella talks about Bobby at Karen's funeral: "Bobby is the only one of them who doesn't have a ***cumare***." This is spelled different ways but still refers to a girl on the side who understands that her guy is a married man.

Sil' is exhibiting more anger at the horse stable: "***Mulligans*** got Martin Luther King day. What do we got? He is inferring that black people have gotten more respect then the Italians.

Jennifer Melfi speaks about Tony with her ex-husband Richard, at his house: "Could he be scared with Albini's Adagio?" She's referring to a baroque Venetian opera composer. Maybe he is just scared of the upper-class Italians.

Sil and Tony are in the car talking about Columbus during the Columbus Day Parade: "A ***medigan*** like him, they fucked everybody else." A ***medigan*** is a pure American that treats outsiders from other cultures like trash.

Sil speaks of his parents, in the car with Tony: "My parents got spit on because they were from ***Calabreeze***." He's referring to Calabrese, a region in southern Italy.

Season 4 Episode 4 - "The Weight"

Ralphie and Tony talk about John at Tony's desk: "Who does he think he is, ***Sir Walter Raleigh***?" He's talking about the famed English courtier who tried to colonize Virginia.

Junior is on his couch talking to Tony: "Making a fortune working with that ***mulligan***." He's saying that he can still make money with black people.

Furio talks to Carmella in the driveway of his new house: "Next year I'll grow grapes for ***Falanghina***." This is a yearly celebration for wine enthusiasts.

Season 4 Episode 5 - "Pie-O-My"

Ralphie is at the Waldorf Astoria for a horse show; "This ***ciccio***, he sells me a horse." ***Ciccio*** in this context means "idiot".

Tony speaks his mind at the track: "Half of these ***cidrules*** live one day to the next." Again, ***cidrules*** (or ***shadrools***) means shit heads or cucumbers.

Ralphie talks to Tony at the stables: "Fluke, ***escolar***, whatever the fuck". Escolar is a harpooned fish.

Chris talks to Adriana in their apartment while she is still in bed: "Do you think Paulie and his ***goomars*** ever get invited to dinner with them?" He is talking about how Paulie's women are too low class to even be invited to a dinner.

In the bar, Bobby meets with the union guy, Teddy Genaretti, of Local 184. Bobby, orders a Wild Turkey, ***neat***. Again, the term ***neat*** means just alcohol, nothing else, no ice. It is a manly word that's use is slowly dying out due to the fact that most men can't drink like that any more.

Bobby gets an earful from Junior while he watches T.V.: "I'm fucking fodder for cartoonists now." Fodder literally means feed for livestock. Junior doesn't like being the brunt of jokes, now that his legal troubles are all over the local news.

Season 4 Episode 6 - "Everybody Hurts"

At Ralphie's house, Artie has to hear this: "Whoa, Chef ***Osso Bucco***." This refers to an Italian dish consisting of braised veal shanks in white wine. It's like Ralphie saying, "Oh, Mr. Fancy Chef is here."

Ralphie continues to insult Artie about his restaurant: "You must be sitting on money like ***King Croesus***." He's referring to an ancient King.

Artie talks to Tony about his daughter at Artie's house: "If Mellissa had a tumor instead of an over-bite, ***modoun*** Santo." With this use of the slang ***modoun***, Artie is saying, "I don't know what I would do", or "it would be the end."

At Artie's restaurant, Charmaine asks: "She suddenly wants to play hide the ***boudin blanc*** with you?" Boudin (pronounced boo-dan), is a highly seasoned link sausage of white pork, pork liver and rice that is a typical element of Louisiana French cuisine. This is another reference to a man's penis.

Tony and Janice have dinner together at Artie's restaurant: "Tony, can I have a ***nonino picolit***?" That is a dessert.

Artie talks to himself in the mirror: "I called you five times, qu' est- ce que cest? Stand up you frog eating ***faccia di cazz***." Translation: What is this, what is this? He wants the frog eating cock sucker to stand up. I guess he doesn't like the French guy…

Artie talks to Tony at the hospital: "Somebody mentions 50,000 to bankroll a French ***digestil***." A ***digestil*** is a beverage, usually small and alcoholic, which is consumed at the end of a meal to aid digestion.

Season 4 Episode 7 - "Watching Too Much Television"

Ralphie and Tony wake up in the front room of the Bing after partying all night: "Oh, ***aspetta***, I'll go with you." Ralphie is saying, "Oh wait, I'll go..."

Tony talks to Cousin Brian at breakfast: "I read about these ***forgase*** mortgage loans." ***Forgase*** means fake or phony.

Chris talks to Adriana about getting married at City Hall: "City Hall, what are we ***schvugs***? A ***schvug*** is a dark lake dweller - another insulting term for people of color.

Season 4 Episode 8 - "Mergers and Acquisitions"

Tony orders dessert for the table at Artie's restaurant: "We'll have one ***Zabaglione*** and 4 spoons." This is a dessert made from egg, cream and custard.

Ro hears from Carmella at the church fund raiser: "You know I put up with this ***goomar*** shit." Carmella tolerates Tony's girlfriends.

Season 4 Episode 9 - "Whoever Did This"

Ralphie gets Paulie's mother, Nucci, all upset about the crank phone call: "***Modoun***, I have blue cross blue shield." In this case ***modoun*** means don't worry. Junior talks to Tony while he is in the hospital bed: "Not Tommy, you ***cidrule***...the son Tommy." In this case, ***cidrule*** means dumb shithead.

Tony gives Junior advice on how to escape his legal dilemma: "All you gotta do is act ***ubatz***." He is saying that Junior should pretend to act senile.

At his home, Junior talks to Tony and Bobby: "Now I have to pretend I'm a fucking idiot ***scumbari.*** My mind has to disappear." Junior feels that he has to pretend that he is mentally impaired. Scumbari means low-life or scumbag.

Ralphie reacts to Pie-o-my's death: "Oh ***modoun***, oh Jesus." In this case ***modoun*** means "oh my God."

Chris and Tony carry Ralph's dead body. Chris remarks: "You're acting like I'm some kind of ***skeeve*** junkie." In this instance, ***skeeve*** means sleazy.

Season 4 Episode 10 - "The Strong and Silent Type"

WOW, THIS WAS THE ONLY EPISODE THAT NOTHING QUESTIONABLE WAS FOUND!

Season 4 Episode 11 - "Calling All Cars"

Tony rambles at Dr. Melfi's office: "Maybe it's this, maybe it's that. Maybe it's ***fungule***." Maybe it's fucking nothing.

Beansie enjoys a massage while he is on the phone with Tony: "I'm in fine fettle." Beansie is saying that he is in good spirits.

Once again, Dr. Melfi attempts therapy in her office. Tony becomes agitated: "You'll cover my 300 a week in no time with some other ***mortadella***." This is slang for meat head or idiot.

Tony enjoys a fine Miami restaurant with Little Carmine. Tony: "You have to feel out your old man so he doesn't give you a ***mazz***." He doesn't want the old man to give him a problem.

Tony speaks through the screen door in his dream: "Me no speak a de English, ***mi dispiace***." I apologize, I'm sorry.

Season 4 Episode 12 - "Eloise"

Furio compliments Carmella's cooking: "***Modoun***, it's like the smell of heaven." In this case ***modoun*** means incredible.

Tony, speaking to Furio in the car: "***Mafungu***, I don't know why I bother." He is saying fuck you, or fuck this conversation.

Little Carmine talks to Big Carmine at the golf course: "He's a bit of a ***posoye*** if you ask me." This is someone who is soft or soupy.

Nucci is in the hospital waiting room with Paulie: "Ah Paulie, ***modoun***." In this case, ***modoun*** means - please, not now.

Meadow cooks dinner in her new apartment. Meadow's roommate tells everyone that she has a "special" family. Meadow responds, "Technically I'm an ***infante de grasia***." She is saying that she is privileged, the infant of grace.

Season 4 Episode 13 - "White Caps"

Little Carmine and Tony have an outdoor meeting: "Whatever kind of acrimony is in the air…" Little Carmine shows off his vocabulary and almost gets a word right.

Tony wises off to Artie at his restaurant: "This is not ***al dente***." This is a term used to describe pasta as under cooked.

Tony's boat, the "Stugots," docks outside the shore house as loud music emanates from the boat's stereo system. The music is Dean Martin from the album "Dino Live at the Sands". This is not just an entertaining scene with great music; but it is extremely funny as well.

The Complete Fifth Season

Tony's separation from Carmela hasn't been working out. His nephew's fiancé has become a distraction. His paroled cousin is giving off bad vibes. His business rival is looking for payback. His therapist isn't buying into the "other Tony." It's enough to send any mob boss over the edge. Hell hath no fury like The Sopranos.

Season 5 Episode 1 - "Two Tonys"

In front of the Bada Bing, Paulie tells Chris about beating someone: "What a beating we gave this cocksucker, ***modoun***." In this case ***modoun*** means it was indescribable.

Chris talks to Adriana about Sil': "Silvio's ***shearole*** we could have got." This is a way of saying money or vegetables or escarole. I think he meant money.

Tony yells at Carmella about the broken coffee maker. "Last month it was the upstairs toilet, ***basta***." He means, enough already.

At Junior's house, Bobby talks about Feech La Mana's prison term: "20 years, ***modoun***." In this case it means, "Can you believe that?"

Tony toasts Feech at Junior's house: "Welcome home, ***chin dann'***." Again, live for one hundred years.

At the Soprano house Benny tells Carmella to bring out the heavy artillery in case the bear comes back. "Open the

closet and give me the ***shkupit.***" This means anything Russian. He really wanted the AK47 Russian assault rifle.
Season 5 Episode 2 - "Rat Pack"

At the funeral home, Chris gives props to a female head of the family: "Lady ***Shylark***, you have some reputation." Her name isn't Lady Shylark. A ***shylark*** is an unlicensed money lender that charges way too much interest. Some may call them a loan shark.

At Big Carmine's funeral, Little Carmine gives John a piece of his mind: "It's for ***Opus Dei*** isn't it." ***Opus Dei*** is the most controversial group in the Catholic Church today with close ties to the Vatican.

Tony comments on a baby picture of himself and his cousin Tony: "Even then my ***Cannolli*** was bigger." He believes his penis has always been more to talk about.

Tony makes a speech at Artie's restaurant: "He passed away, ***buon anima***." It just means "rest his soul," but it's more effective if you do it as a toast.

Tony II (Blundetto), makes fun of Tony S. in front of the guys: "Reginald Van Gleason the Third, m'boy are you fat." This was a poor attempt at an impression of Jackie Gleason doing his famous character Reginald Van Gleason. Jackie, the comic genius, is tough to imitate.

In the back of the Bing, Angelo says to Tony, "I remembered that your ***goomar*** lives there." He is referring to Tony's girlfriend.

Season 5 Episode 3 - "Where's Johnny?"

In the back of the Bing, Tony offers food to Bobby: "Want some coffee...***bialy***?" A ***bialy*** is a type of bagel that is little known outside the N.J. and N.Y area.

Aunt Mary tells Paulie about the gardener: "Off ***modoun***, someone beat up the gardener." In this case it means, "Have you heard?"

At Feech's bakery office, Paulie gets told off: "Your book don't mean ***oogotz*** to me." He is saying that it is worth nothing to him. What a meanie.

At Sunday dinner, Tony asks for food to be passed to him: 'Hey pass the ***regatta***." He is saying ricotta cheese.

Tony and John meet outside at a park: "Having Phil Leotardo smack your ***shys*** around is not the smartest thing." Tony is referring to the people that owe him money as being shy, or short of paying him. You play, you pay.

Tony talks about Junior on the phone with Bobby: "He can wander off the ***Palisades*** for all I care." Palisades is a town in Jersey that used to have a famous carnival park with a boardwalk.

Tony yells at Janice concerning her voicing her grievances: "Poor fucking Janice, ***va fongul***." This is the bad way of saying fuck you. Not a lot of slang there.

Season 5 Episode 4 - "All The Happy Families"

Feech talks to Tony about Adriana: "Tommy Pinto's ***goomar***, when I was coming up, had legs up to here." He's comparing Tommy Pinto's girlfriend to Adriana.

Sil' talks to Tony about Feech: "He's a ***strunz***." This is a tough old timer. It can also mean an old strong rock of shit.

Tony makes fun of Feech at the card game. "….and it falls off and she keels over, ***che puzz***." This means, "oh, what a stink."

Season 5 Episode 5 - "Irregular Around The Margins"

Tony tells Adriana about the Band-Aid on his head: "It's cancer, yeah ***squamous***." ***Squamous*** is not Jersey slang or an Italian word, but I thought you might like to know that it means skin cancer. I didn't know either.

In the office of the Bada Bing, Chris yells at Tony: "Everyone knows you have been the biggest fucking ***cooze*** hound the past four or five years." He means Tony is a man in search of pussy and more pussy.

In the back room, the boys make fun of Vito's penis: "Then you have a problem because your ***brojoll*** is not that long." As most men do, they find a food to compare their penis to. I can't eat brojolli without laughing.

Season 5 Episode 6 - "Sentimental Education"

Carmella and the Priest talk in the restaurant: "Maybe you should send the ***Papel Nuncio*** to Tony and remind him of that." She sarcastically recommends that he sends the Pope himself.

Vito and Paulie discuss Cousin Tony's massage business: You really ***scheave*** the human body don't you?" This word has many meanings but in this case, Vito is inferring that he thinks Paulie finds the human body to be disgusting.

Cousin Tony finds a lot of money. He tells the boys about it at the Bing. Sil remarks, "72 grand, ***modoun a mia***." Sil' is saying, "oh my Madonna, that's a lot of money." And he's right.

In his car, Paulie tells Cousin Tony what he's going to do: "I'm gonna ***mange*** and hit the sack for the next 14 hours." Before he goes to sleep he's going to get a bite to eat.

In A.J.'s classroom, the teacher, Tom Fisk, tells Robert Wegler what he thinks about A.J.'s grades at school: "Fredo Corleone can get a C 'cause you asked." He is making a reference to the movie, The Godfather. He is comparing A.J. to the character Fredo. Neither son was the smartest of the family…

Season 5 Episode 7 - "In Camelot"

In the gym, Chris takes J.T.'s bet: "You take a ***dime*** each on the Yankees and St. Louis?" A ***dime*** is $1000 in gambling terms.

Hesh talks to Tony about Johnny Soprano's girlfriend: "Oh, I should give it to some trollop." This is a dirty or untidy woman.

J.T. is upset with Chris at the poker game: "You charging me a ***vig***?" A ***vig*** is the percentage on top of the principle that is charged as long as the debt remains unpaid.

In the real world they make it sound nice by saying "interest". I always thought that there was nothing interesting about interest.

A flashback of Johnny and Olivia Soprano in the hospital: "***Modoun***, we got home and saw that note. I got scared." In this case Johnny meant that he felt helpless.

Sil talks to Tony at the Bing: "Hesh tells me that you met your father's ***goomar***." In this case the ***goomar*** was a woman that stayed with Tony's father her whole life. She was dedicated to him even though he was married to another woman.

Season 5 Episode 8 - "Marco Polo"

Tony and John look at the new Maseratti: "Phil ***modoun a me***, he won't let go." He is saying, "Oh my God, enough." The slang "modoun" originates from the name Madonna; the holy mother.

Junior is on the phone with Hugh, Carmela's father: "I wanna wish you a ***buona fortuna***." Good fortune on your birthday.

Cousin Tony speaks to Tony S. in the back of the Bada Bing: "I'm a team player. I'm ***Charlie Hustle***." I just hope Soprano fans realize that this is an expression used when referring to the all time hit leader, Pete Rose. (That's "hit," as in baseball)

Cousin Tony and Rusty have dinner. Rusty explains: "A friend of a friend, not a friend of ours." That means that the man he is referring to is not made and can't be trusted completely.

Carmella is on the phone with Tony and she is talking about her dad: "The New York salsicc." This is another way of saying sausage.

Phil looks over his repaired car at the body shop with Tony B: "You can sit in there until fucking ***San Gennaro***." San Gennaro of Benevento was an Italian saint. They are talking about the San Gennaro festival, held once a year.

Everyone is poolside at Hugh's birthday party. Father Phil talks to Dr. Russ: "An Italian allergic to ***pommedori***? Dio, mio." Loosely translated: "My God, an Italian that can't eat tomatoes?" Makes sense, huh?

At poolside, Carmella's mother talks about Olivia: "Olivia detested northern cooking, she ***skeeved*** the butter." Apparently she found butter to be disgusting.

Carmella's mom asks if anyone is hungry: "***Bollito misto, osso bucco, fritt misto, bacala***." She's offering boiled fish, veal shank, fried fish and salted cod fish. It looks better then it sounds.

Carmella talks in the driveway with her mother: "Didn't want to meet your ***gavone*** son-in-law?" Carmela implies that her mom thinks Tony is a scumbag.

Season 5 Episode 9 - "Unidentified Black Males"

John and Tony talk about the late Joey Peeps: "I picked him out of the chorus." John is saying that he was hand picked and special.

In Dr. Melfi's office, Tony speaks well of himself: "But I'm no ***gabadotz*** myself." He means he is not lazy or a hard headed slacker.

At the construction site, Gene talks about a necklace: "The necklace, how'd it go over with the ***goomar***?" Did your girlfriend like it?

Meadow talks about her family at dinner with Finn: "From the poverty of ***Mezzogiorno***." This is referring to a poor region of Southern Italy.

Tony relates a story about himself and Tony B. at Dr. Melfi's office: "I was jumped by a bunch of *moolinyans*." He literally said that eggplants jumped him, but I am pretty sure he means black people. Who originated that bad slang word?

Season 5 Episode 10 - "Cold Cuts"

Tony talks to Chris on the way to Uncle Pat's farm: "….and water his tomatoes and his basinigol." It seems that Uncle Pat liked to grow his own Basil.

Season 5 Episode 11 - "The Test Dream"

Tony B's mom is on the phone with Tony S: "Modoun, I was hoping he was with you." She is saying "oh no, now I'm worried." Also it's a quick prayer to ask for help from the Madonna, the Holy Mother.

In Artie's restaurant, the actress Annette Bening makes a reference to the movie The Godfather: "I don't want my husband to come out of there with just his cock in his hand." In the Godfather movie, the character Sonny said that about his brother Mike when he was on his way to shoot a cop in the restaurant.

Season 5 Episode 12 - "Long Term Parking"

Little Carmine has an interesting way of saying that they are stagnating and can't get anything done: "We are in a fuckin' ***stagmire***." He means "quagmire". Little Carmine is notorious for his misuse of words in the series.

Chris walks into the back of the Crazy Horse: "The highway was jammed with broken heroes on a last chance power drive." This is a line from Bruce Springsteen's "Born to Run". Originally from Freehold, Bruce is the King of Jersey. While we're on the subject, I recommend that you hear the hardest working man in Jersey, Southside Johnny.

At the sit down, Johnny's boys calm him down: "Jimmy's right, ***aspetta***." He means: wait, please think clearly.

Artie is serving dinner to Carmella and Tony: "Little Meadow in a bridal gown, modoun." In this case modoun means that he can't believe it.

Chris and Adriana are at their apartment talking about Tony: "You cost him a dime, you're a fucking pariah." A pariah is an outcast.

Season 5 Episode 13 - "All Due Respect"

Everyone raises their glasses to Raymond at the restaurant to celebrate his birthday: "***Buon natal, cent' ann***." Happy birthday and may there be one hundred more.

Tony and Vito are at the same dinner. "***Vito misto***, how are you?" He is asking Tony respectfully, "Are you mixed up or stressed out?"

Chris talks to Sil' through his car window: "And I'm supposed to take a bullet for the ***skeeve***?" In this case skeeve means a vile person.

At his house, Junior talks to Tony: "He'll sound a little ***stunoda***, maybe forever." This means he will talk slow and sound stupid.

Sil' to Tony: "We got you a Bialy and coffee." Bialy is a type of bagel that is popular in Jersey and New York and no one knows why it never made it much further than that.

Johnny Sack and Tony are on the phone to set up a meeting: "You think I'm gonna give you ***armatz*** with Ginny upstairs? Johnny doesn't want Tony to worry about being put to death or having his hand cut off. Johnny would never do that with his wife Ginny upstairs.

Tony talks to John outside in the snow: "You wanna eat K-rations? - fine." These were the military's way of feeding the troops. He's referring to canned food.

Tony's lawyer, Neil, reminds Tony how bad things can be: "It's a major ***kreplach*** my friend." Kreplach are small noodles or dumplings filled with ground meat, usually boiled and served in chicken soup. They are similar to Italian ravioli or often referred to as Jewish wontons. Kreplach is a traditional Jewish dish often served on the day before Yom Kippor (the Day of Atonement) or on Hoshana Rabbah (the 7th day of the Festival of Booths).

The Complete Sixth Season

Several crises threaten Tony and his crew; for starters, rival boss Johnny Sack (Vince Curatola) is in prison, and the always-tense relations between the New Jersey and New York families are strained through the unpredictable behavior of Sack's surrogates. Then there are the inevitable power struggles that ensue when certain family members are eliminated.... by natural and other causes.

Season 6 Part I, Episode 1 - "Members Only"

Tony discusses Gino's future: "You took an oath." Tony is telling Gino that he is a made man. Gino reminds him: "There was ***Joey Bananas***." He is referring to Joe Bonanno, a real ex -New York mobster that was allowed to leave the mob for a cash settlement.

In this episode, Tony sits at a restaurant with his back to the window. Everyone knows a gangster is normally too paranoid to do that. This is not the only time he does it.

Outside Satrialie's, Phil addresses Vito: "***Cugino mio***." He is saying, "hello my good cousin."

In the hospital, Tony talks to Hesh: "Talk to Phil about this ***mook***..." A mook is a dummy that tries but just doesn't understand his surroundings.

In Artie's restaurant, the conversation shifts to Vito: "The antipast." He is saying antipasto. Paulie says: "He's a ***studaod*** of the first magnitude." He is saying that he is stupider than stupid.

In the funeral home, Tony talks to Rusty (played by Frankie Valli): "W.R.A.T. another on now." Tony is talking of still another gangster that is informing the F.B.I. of their illegal activities. It's as if it was broadcast on a radio station. He's got a lot of nerve.

Season 6 Part I, Episode 2 - "Join The Club"

At the hospital, Paulie tells Vito that it's his turn to do a favor: "You already brought the ***sfogliatelle***." Vito brought pastries for everyone at the hospital.

At Geno's funeral, Vito talks about how Junior shot Tony: "He Marvin Gayed his nephew." The popular singer, Marvin Gaye, was shot and killed by his own father. I heard it through the grape vine.

Still at the funeral home, Paulie reminds us that Junior has been around for a long time and deserves respect: "Roseville has been Junior's territory since the big bang."

Season 6 Part I, Episode 3 - "Mayhem"

Paulie complains about the drug dealer robbery and about the lack of cash: "***Oogatz*** here." He means that there is not enough money to justify the robbery.

At the hospital Meadow greets Chris: "***Cugin***." Hey Cousin.

In the hospital waiting room Vito says: "***Ava Napoli***" and Bobby responds: "Mari, what that ***miserab*** admitted to you." Vito is paying homage to the old country and Naples, and Bobby is saying that it is a miserable attitude to have.

Paulie gets a little antsy with Vito: "Back up there, ***Bluto***." That's Paulie's way of calling Vito fat. Bluto was a rather large character in the Popeye cartoons. Toot, toot. Sing the song if you know it.

At the hospital waiting room, Vito talks about how tough it is for Silvio: "Sil's on the canvas now." He is making a reference to a boxing match. The floor of the boxing ring is made from canvas.

Paulie walks into the ICU at the hospital for the first time and sees Tony: "Oof ***modoun***, he looks terrible." In this case, ***modoun*** means: "oh my god, he looks terrible."

Still in the ICU, Paulie talks to Tony who is in a coma: That fucking ***agita***, T." This word has many meanings and Paulie uses them all. In this case, Paulie is complaining about how upsetting his life is. He has unnecessary frustrations....meanwhile; it's Tony that's in a coma...

In Vito's house, Paulie tells Vito that Tony woke up from his coma: "He's conscious, you ***capisce***?" Or, "do you understand?"

Season 6 Part I, Episode 4 - "The Fleshy Part of The Thigh"

Paulie goes to see his aunt Dottie in the hospital. He sees her naked legs exposed and covers them with the sheets: "Ah ooh, ***modoun*** Aunt Dottie, hold on a second." This word has many meanings. Paulie has used most of them. He is not covering her legs for respect. He is saying that he doesn't need to see an old lady's ugly legs in the nicest way he can. In this case he is right. Those legs should always be covered up.

Season 6 Part I, Episode 5 - "Mr. and Mrs. John Sacrimoni Request"

In the back of Satrialie's, Tony shows his stomach scar to Chris: "Ahh modoun check this scar out." Chris is saying "holy mackerel, this is a big one." Again, this word has many different meanings, and is used in many contexts.

At the back room at Satrialie's during a poker game, Tony talks to his new bodyguard: "***Penne arabratta*** peppers up his ass." If you haven't figured, these are very hot peppers.

In the parking lot, Tony talks to Phil: "You have more buttons then my grandmother's corsets." He means he has more made men in his crew then anyone else. The more made men there are the more untouchable the crew is.

At Allegra's wedding, Tony asks A.J. about his future: "Hey ***googootz,*** you wanna be an event planner?' ***Googootz*** is really a squash or a pumpkin, but you can talk down to someone and use it as a way of calling someone a punk. Someone of higher status cannot be referred to in this way.

At Allegra's wedding, Chris makes a reference to the first Godfather movie. To Tony: "Like the movie, ***One***, you can't refuse a man's request on his wedding day."

At the gay bar, the # 1 collections guy, Sal, gives his opinion of the place: "Fucking ***scheeve*** this shit." He is disgusted just being around the people in the bar. Sal is quite homophobic.

Season 6 Part I, Episode 6 - "Live Free or Die"

In the Bada Bing, Paulie talks about Vito's homosexuality: "He's a married man with a ***goomar***." Even Vito kept a girlfriend on the side to create the illusion that he was one of the boys.

In the back room of the Bada Bing, Tony talks about Vito: "You knew he was a ***recchion***?" It's a way of calling someone a fag. It is usually accompanied by a pull on the ear. This is a sign to the other person that you mean he is a real fag and it is not just an expression.

Still in the back room, Paulie shows his homophobia: "Maybe you are a ***flambee***." In the back room, Tony talks to Chris about the Arabs: "Those two Arabs, ***fazool*** or whatever his name is." More disrespect.

At Vito's shore house, Benny lets him know that Tony needs to see him: "Fucking ***fanook***." They are convinced that he is a fag.

At Artie's restaurant, Carmella talks to Angie: "Two thousand dollars? ***modoun***, Angie." She expresses that that's a lot of money.

Talking about Vito to Rae, Carmella uses the Italian word for fag: "Those kids, to find out their father is a ***fanook***."

In Satriale's back room, Chris tells what he would do to Vito: "Cut off his ***pisat pisciattill***, and feed it to him." He suggests that he cut off his Pee-Pee.

At Tony's desk, Silvio talks about Paulie's view of Vito: "He is going ***mau-mau*** over the subject." Silvio means Paulie is going ballistic over the fact that Vito is gay.

At Tony's desk, Silvio continues to talk about Vito: "Let's say the guy shows up. You gonna kiss him on both cheeks?" Kissing a man on both checks is a sign of full respect for a made man. Although a kiss on the lips is a sign of death.

Season 6 Part I, Episode 7 - "Luxury Lounge"

At Artie's restaurant, Phil fits in a beauty: "But this with the ***agro dolce***...." He means sweet and sour tasting.

While walking in the parking lot with Tony, Chris tells Tony how he is looking for Vito by visiting his girlfriend: "Paid a visit to his goomar, Jill." Remember, a goomar is a girl on the side.

In the new Italian restaurant, Giovanni's, Carmella complements the food: "Just a scoop of cool regutta." "Regutta" is ricotta cheese.

In Giovanni's restaurant, Phil is surprised how careful Tony is: "***Modoun***, are you a cautious man." In his position, Phil doesn't think Tony needs to be that careful.

In Arties restaurant waiting bar, Artie gets Benny another drink. "Get the man another ***buca***." I guess Benny was drinking Sambuca, a licorice flavored alcohol that is served after dinner with three coffee beans in it.

Poolside with Ben Kingsley, Carmine Tazzi pitches the movie idea: "Logline, The Ring meets The Godfather."

A logline is an industry term that means one or two lines to describe a movie script.

At Tony's desk, Benny tells him that his wife is pregnant with a boy: "I saw his ***cannoli*** on the ultra sound like last month." If you have ever seen a cannoli, you've noticed that it is shaped like a good sized male member. If you have never seen a cannoli, it is a cream filled, penis shaped dessert.

At Artie's restaurant, Benny's family makes a toast: "***Chent ann***." This is an Italian toast that means "live for one hundred years." So, salut.

In Artie's kitchen, Artie yells at one of his employees: "Like icing on a cake okay, capisce?" "Capisce" means understand.

Season 6 Part I, Episode 8 - "Johnny Cakes"

Outside Satrialie's, Tony speaks with Chris and Sil: "I have a ***baguette*** 24/7." A baguette is a long thin loaf of French bread. Tony is proud of his hard-on.

In Satrialie's, Tony explains to the Jamba Juice woman about the neighborhood: "My family made the trip from the ***guinea gulch***." Tony refers to the Italians that came from the bottom of the food chain. "My father came from Avelino." That is a town just outside of Naples in Italy.

Tony takes a walk in his neighborhood: "Hey Mrs. Conte, ***como esta***?" He just is asking how she is doing today.

Tony visits the grocery store in the old neighborhood: "So how's business? ***Messa mezza***?" This great expression means "so-so".

In the New York nightclub, A.J.'s club buddy speaks of Tony's status: "***Capo di tutti capi***." He shows respect for Tony but not his son. He says, I understand that he is the notorious head of all.

At an outdoor meeting with Phil and Tony, Phil reminds Tony of what his father would do: "A ***finook*** in his crew, he knew how to handle that." Phil doesn't think a fag should be in Tony's crew.

A club girl giving A.J. a back massage asks a few questions: "You know, ***omertà***." Omertà is a popular attitude, common in areas of southern Italy, such as Sicily, Calabria and Campania, where the criminal organizations like the Mafia, 'Ndrangheta and Camorra are strong. Omertà implies "the categorical prohibition of cooperation with state authorities or reliance on its services, even when one has been victim of a crime." Even if somebody is convicted of a crime he has not committed, he is supposed to serve the sentence without giving the police any information about the real criminal. A common definition is the code of silence. Within Mafia culture, breaking the oath of omertà is punishable by death.

Season 6 Part I, Episode 9 - "The Ride"

In church, Paulie talks to the new priest: "In a couple of days Joe Vella will be by with the ***flow***." A gangster always finds new words for money.

Tony and Chris sit and eat at the restaurant and discuss the wine theft from the Vipers: "How about that prick's face when he saw the ***gat***." Tony replaces the word gun for gat.

At the Soprano dinner table, Chris talks about a lot of money: "El mucho pesos."

The Emcee at the St. Elzear's festival starts the cannoli eating contest: "Ready set, ***mangia***." Mangia is Italian for "eat". Saint Elzear is the saint of the household.

Paulie hears his mother complain about him at the festival: "You need to make a ***Novena***, Paulie." In the Catholic Church, a Novena is a nine day private or public devotion to help absolve sin and obtain special graces.

In the bathroom, Paulie tells Tony about his biopsy: "I'd rather face 10 guys with ***shivs*** then something I can't see." A shiv is a home-made knife, usually found in prison.

Season 6 Part I, Episode 10 - "Moe n' Joe"

Vito cooks for Johnny Cakes. "We got a little ***zalad***." He is serving a salad with the meal. It's not a special dessert.

In the Soprano kitchen, Carmella talks to Meadow: "You put the ***cevedell*** in?" Did you put the sausage in the oven?

Season 6 Part I, Episode 11 - "Cold Stones"

Tony and Carmella in their kitchen talk about the French people: "But the frogs hate us." Tony calls the French "frogs" because as a Republican, he knows that the French do not get along with Americans at this time.

Tony watches T.V. and talks about the character in the movie: "Speaking of crystal meth, look at this ***walyo***." A walyo is someone who is tripping on drugs.

Vito sees a customer in the supermarket: "***Hey, hop along che-se-ditch***." This is a sarcastic greeting as if to say, "how ya doin cowboy."

Tony meets Phil at the Lou Costello statue in Hoboken N.J. where the comic genius of Abbott & Costello fame was from: "Heard on 10-10 WINS the tunnel's a parking lot." "10-10 WINS" is the local news radio station." Phil answers, "You said you were gonna take care of the fuckin' ***finook***." He is talking about Vito the fag, or finook.

In the back of Satrialie's, Bobby talks about Vito's death: "A cop up there told me, ***minchia***." Derived from the Italian for penis, Minchia is used as a noun describing ANYTHING that is cheesy, stereotypical, self-conscious or just plain minchia. In this case it means "dick", as in: "he didn't tell me dick" (he didn't tell me anything). This definition is minchia in and of itself.

In the French restaurant, Rosalie sees the food arrive: "Oof modoun." She is saying that the meal looks fantastic.

Dom Gamillo shows up at the back room with Sil': "They are the pirates of ***prosciutt***." This is slang for Prosciutto, an Italian dried ham or pork.

After killing Dom, Sil' gives directions: "Ditch his car and get some ***biangaleen***." Sil thinks that bleach will do the trick.

In the garage, A.J. gets a "heart to heart" from Tony: "You got hooded sweatshirts like the ***mulligans*** wear that you watch on T.V." He is talking about how A.J. emulates the rappers he watches in black music videos.

Season 6 Part I, Episode 12 - "Kaisha"

Benny and Tony on the phone talk about the explosion: "Your friend the Shah was walking in when it happened. He and some ***skifusa*** got blown on their keesters." Benny remembers that Tony thinks Phil looks like the Shah of Iran. A skifusa is someone who looks like they got kicked in the head.

Tony talks to Chris at the Thanksgiving football game. "I know you have a new goomar." He knows that Chris has a new girlfriend.

In Dr. Melfi's office, Tony talks about the women in his life: "There's you and Gloria and this ***Ashkenazi***." He means the real state agent - a Russian Jew.

Chris is on the phone with his wife who is dictating a shopping list: "Bring me a ***Quattro Formaggi***. I don't care how late it is." That is a dish comprised of a four cheese sauce that is served over pasta. If not made right, it can be too cheesy. But when it is made right, Fu- geh-da-bow-dit!

At the Soprano Christmas, A.J.s new girl friend hears compliments about the new jewel around her neck. "Hey that is quite a ***bagatelle***." From the Italian *bagatella* - meaning a small piece of property.

Season 6 Part 2, Episode 1 - "Soprano Home Movies"

Tony's comes home from his brief stay in prison. Paulie is at Tony's house waiting for him: "Take the yellow ribbon down, he's home." Tying a yellow ribbon around an old oak tree is an ancient tradition meant to honor returning soldiers from distant wars. The ribbon is meant to symbolize that your spouse or your family still yearn for your return, and to not walk past the house where they are waiting.

Tony and Bobby shoot a fully automatic weapon in the woods: "Modoun, the power": Tony is saying, "Wow, this is some gun!"

In the lake house kitchen, Carmella tells Janice that she's concerned about Tony's excessive drinking: "Tony seems to hit the ***hooch*** a little hard at lunch." Hooch is a slang word for a home made whiskey that is made solely for the purpose of getting drunk, sort of like moonshine. It's also a slang word for alcohol, you know - booze. This is not a Jersey term at all.

On the boat, Tony complements Bobby: "You never popped your cherry in that regards, ah, salute"- referring to the fact that Bobby never was asked to perform a "hit" - to kill someone. This is considered rare that an experienced Mafioso has never been asked before, and Tony congratulates him.

At the lake house during dinner, Carmela and Janice toast: "Chend ann, Anthony." "Chend ann" is a toast meaning "may you live a hundred years."

At the lake house over a game of Monopoly, Janice tells a story of her mother "driving back from Manhattan with Uncle Junior and his "***goomar.***" A "goomar" is a slang word for a man's mistress or girlfriend - usually the girl he's seeing behind his wife's back.

The scene shifts to the girls sitting at the beach by the lake house. Janice tells Carmella about her father. "He was Neapolitan to the core." She is saying that her father followed the traditions of his ancestors from Naples his whole life.

Tony meets with some Canadian mobsters at a restaurant near the lake house: "That's tough talk, ***bon ami***." Tony is saying "you are my good friend."

Season 6 Part 2, Episode 2 - "Stage 5"

In the movie "Cleaver" (Chris's stab at movie-making) the actor in the movie speaks: "***Nafuncciis***" - meaning; wow, don't nag me.

At the Badabing, Silvio tells Tony: "Chrissie is the last guy I'd confuse with Marty." Martin Scorsese is referred to as Marty by the Italians who believe they can relate to him, as if he is one of them.

In the restaurant, just before the shooting, Silvio relates: "We had a ***quarto gatti***": A meeting conducted around a dinner table. This is considered proper protocol.

In the back room the crew drinks to the recent passing of John Sacrimoni: "***Buen anima***." (May he rest in peace).

Phil talks about his immediate family's life as he sits at the bar: "My family took shit from the ***medigans*** from the time they got off the boat." The "medigans" refers to American's that treated the people migrating from other counties like trash.

Season 6 Part 2, Episode 3 - "Remember When"

In a Virginia sports bar, Paulie talks about Tony's father: "Your dad had to ***duke*** to get a hundred fuckin dollars." Paulie assures Tony that his dad worked or fought hard to get his money, even for just a small sum.

In the minimum security prison recreation room, Junior insults the other people: "Don't feed the ***chedrulls*** (shadrools)."

In a Miami restaurant Paulie, acting like the scum that he is, talks about Beansie: "Uff, ***modoun***, he pisses in a bag now" - Paulie's way of saying "Oh my God, can you believe this guy can't even use the bathroom like the rest of us" - (the man is impaired and has a tube connected to his bladder).

Still in the Miami restaurant, Beansie tells a story about Paulie's past: "This guy throws a vat of hot oil from a ***zeppole*** stand." Zeppoles or zeeplas are an Italian pastry resembling an elephant ear. There is always a zeppole stand at local Italian fares and are most often served on holidays. It is tasty fried dough sometimes filled with Italian cheese. I traditionally make them with my niece Alyssa on Christmas Eve.

Tony asks for money while he is on the phone with Hesh: "I need a ***bridge loan***, 200 K." A bridge loan is money borrowed to pay someone else off. And 200 K is two hundred thousand dollars. Yeah, sure, I have it right here on my dresser ...

In the Miami boat yard a Latin mobster addresses Paulie: "Okay, ***tio***." He is calling him uncle.

Tony talks about Paulie to Beansie by the pool: "He's got the ***gazzies*** of a 20 year old." This is Tony's way of saying that Paulie is tough, but with no brains. He continues, "Oh my god what a ***chiacchierone***, he's Gary fucking Cooper": Now Tony is saying that Paulie is way too talkative and overly dramatic - in other words, his storytelling is like that of a bad actor (not that Gary Cooper was a bad actor, mind you). A ***chiacchierone*** is a chatterbox.

Tony and Beansie are still poolside: "Things are going great; maybe I'm waiting for the other foot (shoe) to drop." Tony thinks if he takes another step that his world might come tumbling down - he's waiting for something bad to happen.

Season 6 part 2, Episode 4 - "Chasing It"

Sil and Tony look outside the window at Satrialie's butcher shop: "Off, look at this ***mezza-mort***," referring to Vito's wife. Sil is saying that since the death of Vito, his wife is walking around like she's half dead.

At Hesh's house, Hesh comments to Tony: "Lonely at the top, ***boychick***?" Hesh is sarcastically and rhetorically calling Tony a young man.

In the back room at Satrialie's, the boys are all sitting at a table when Hesh walks in. Paulie greets him: "***Asset***, play a hand." This means more then just sit with us. This is an invitation to bond with the Italians, or hold court and play cards. But with Paulie saying it, you know he has an ulterior motive: he most likely just wants him to lose money at poker.

The boys sit at the black jack table and continue to win: "Enjoy the Borgata." The Borgata Hotel Casino is the newest of the Atlantic City casinos and has quickly established itself as a top hot spot. The Borgata is a slice of Las Vegas in Atlantic City with an Italian village theme. Go any where else? - Fu- geh-da-bow-dit.

Paulie tells a story to the boys at the restaurant: "Cocksucker's Corvair Monza is still in the garage." We know that the Corvair is a car made by Chevy. Monza is a city in northern Italy north-northeast of Milan. It's the ancient capital of Lombardy. So store that away and never use it.

Season 6 Part 2, Episode 5 - "Walk Like A Man"

Paulie discuses business with Chris at the Badda-Bing: "***Modoun***, those belt sanders flyin' off the shelves." In this instance Modoun means that he would have never guessed how well they are doing. Then Paulie tells Chris not to get cunty. Or don't act like a bitchy girl.

Chris storms into the room and approaches Tony's desk. Tony lets him know that he is unhappy about it: "Go have a Lime Rickey or whatever the fuck you're drinking these days." Tony refers to a Lime Rickey as a pansy drink. He's also making fun of Chrissie's new found sobriety. It is a pansy drink except it does have alcohol in it. If I remember correctly from my five years of bartending, a Lime Rickey consists of lime juice, gin, bitters and soda with a lime wedge. It sounds refreshing, but not for a made man.

Jason and the rest of the college boys take bets from Victor in the frat house: "Buffalo's a lock, gimme a ***dime*** and ***two and a half***." Well, Victor sure is kind of young to know that he wants to put $1000 and 2 ½ points on one team to win.

Carmela and Tony talk about Anthony being a miserable person: "It's a pleasure not having him hang around here like a ***miserab'***."

Paulie talks to Chris at the bar: "There is no point in ruminating." Again Paulie tries to use a big word and misuses it. What he means is not to have stale air around them when they are in the same room.

Season 6 Part 2, Episode 6 - "Kennedy & Heidi"

Tony and Chris are in the car and talk about Phil: "He's got us by the ***gotz***." Even though he is referring to their balls, a gotz is more of the hand that's got them. A gotz was supposedly a metal glove worn in the 1600's in Germany. Many men were scared of this hand because it was known for squeezing a man's…well, you know what. Anyway over the years it transferred to just the balls. I don't know if this is true; that's just the legend.

Chris's mother is with Kelly in the Soprano house, holding the baby: "Oh, you little ***shfooyadell***." The grandmother is saying that she could eat the baby up like a pastry. That's a good thing, considering we don't really eat our young.

Season 6 Part 2, Episode 7 - "The Second Coming"

Phil gives Tony an attitude at the sit down: "20 years in the can, I wanted ***mannigut***." That's simply the way we say Manicotti (a dish consisting of large, tubular noodles stuffed with a mild cheese and baked in tomato sauce) and we won't change it.

Meadow sets A.J. straight about the family: "A.J., we are Italian and you are their son. Don't you know what that means? You will always be more important." This explains a lot about the attitude of the whole show. Men are more important because they will take care of the things that women don't understand. I believe the women are the smart ones for letting them believe that. For that matter, the men die before the women and the women get all their stuff. Oh yeah, and who pays for dinner?

In the back of the Bing, Paulie asks Tony if he is hungry: "You hungry? I'll send the kid for Baja Fresh." This is not an Italian slang for some crazy food. It's a struggling Mexican fast food chain that is owned by Wendy's.

Season 6 Part 2, Episode 8 - "The Blue Comet"

Tony orders food at Satrialie's: "***Gabagool***, provolone, vinegar and peppers." The Gabagool is Capicola (Italian lunch meat) for his sub sandwich.

Tony and Silvio in the back room of the Badda Bing: "Come on I just finished my ***bialy***." A bialy is a small roll named for the city of Bialystok in Poland. A traditional bialy is a chewy yeast roll similar to a bagel. Unlike a bagel, a bialy is not boiled; rather, it is simply baked (bagels are boiled before baking), and instead of a hole in the middle it has a depression. Before baking, this depression is filled with diced onions and other ingredients, including (depending on the recipe) garlic, poppy seeds, or bread crumbs. A Bialy is little known out of the N.Y. and Jersey areas.

All of Phil's guys discuss who in the Soprano family should be killed and they refer to Bobby as a mortadel or a meathead. ***Mortadel*** is slang for mortadella - a finely hashed, ground heat-cured pork sausage which incorporates lardoons of pork fat.

Bobby gives Paulie information at Silvio's desk: "Phil's at his ***goomar*** every Friday night." Bobby is referring to Phil's Ukrainian girlfriend.

Paulie is worried at the Bing bar: "Don't discuss this until we're in the ***pescia dun***." Pescia dun is an Italian commune fort, or a safe house.

In Artie's restaurant, Charmaine offers to bring some ***lemoncellos***. This is a small dessert cake or pastry. It means small lemons.

Tony Tells Sil what he needs everyone to do: "Get a ***20*** on Phil." This is an old C.B. radio or Police band term meaning location.

In the hobby shop right before his murder, Bobby fantasizes about the toy train: "Imagine sitting in the club car sipping on a ***Negroni***." A Negroni is a cocktail made with gin. It's specifically considered an aperitif, or pre-dinner cocktail, intended to stimulate the drinker's appetite. The recipe includes gin, sweet vermouth, Campari, and a twist of orange.

Sil, getting ready to leave the office, is hurriedly packing his stuff from his desk: "All right, ***aspett***." This means, "wait a minute."

The guys finally make it to the safe house: "We order a ***pizz***?" "They want permission to order a pizza.

Season 6 Part 2, Episode 9 - "Made in America"

Tony walks up to Janice on her deck: "***Farraras***." He brought her pan candy (Farraras is the brand name).

The F.B.I agent Harris talks to Tony on the phone: "He's lammed out. He probably can't get a clean cell phone." He is saying that he is on the run and in hiding.

There is lots of tension at the sit down: "We've got a dead g***oomar*** in Queens." A goomar is a girlfriend that under stands that she is with a married man. So, in this instance, it is inferred that she or her family most likely will be taken care of.

Tony asks Meadow about her brother at the restaurant: "What do you think is wrong with ***gagootz***?" This is a term to call someone a punk in a nice way. An Italian can never use this word referring to someone who is equal or above himself. The word's meaning is Italian for pumpkin. I also noticed that Tony was sitting with his back to the window, again. I don't even do that when I can afford to eat out.

Paulie accepts Tony's offer at the table outside of Satriale's: "I live to serve you my liege." He is pledging his allegiance to Tony in his usual, overly dramatic way.

A.J. talks to Carmela while he watches T.V.: "You said we'd be having ***Mannigut***." He thought that she made Manicotti for dinner.

Tony goes to see Uncle Junior and uncle Jun' has an attitude: "Fuck you want....? a ***boutonniere***?" A boutonniere is a French flower or small bunch of flowers worn in a buttonhole on a lapel.

In the last scene Tony sits at the restaurant. "Where's ***gagootz***?" Tony wants to know where his punk son, A.J., is.

Well, that's it. I hope you learned something that you can impress your friends with. If you didn't learn anything it's because you are from Jersey or you didn't pay attention to the show. Either way this book is useful for that special friend that has no idea why you are laughing at parts of the Sopranos that they just can't understand. Just throw the book at them and tell them you're trying to watch the show. So learn yourself something, you ***mamaluke***. Enjoy.

Written by: Danny Paul
Executive Producers: Rama Barwick & Paul Klein
Concept: Paul Klein & Danny Paul
Design: Michael Lauzardo
Project Coordinator: Todd Little

Essential Media Group LLC
1835 East Hallandale Beach Blvd
Suite 621
Hallandale, FL 33009
Phone: (954) 208-0552 Fax: (954) 208 0061
Email: info@essentialmg.com

Made in the USA
Las Vegas, NV
29 May 2022

49526258R00049